Seashore

COLORING BOOK

Jessica Mazurkiewicz

DOVER PUBLICATIONS, INC.
MINEOLA, NEW YORK

Bibliographical Note

Seashore Coloring Book: Your Passport to Calm is a new work, first published by
Dover Publications, Inc., in 2016.

International Standard Book Number
ISBN-13: 978-0-486-81071-3
ISBN-10: 0-486-81071-2

Manufactured in the United States by RR Donnelley
81071201   2016
www.doverpublications.com

bliss

\'blis\

noun

1. supreme happiness; utter joy or contentment

2. heaven; paradise

3. your passport to calm

Take a pleasant journey to a world of relaxation with *BLISS Seashore Coloring Book: Your Passport to Calm*. This treasury features 46 ready-to-color images that will conjure up a tranquil day at the beach, from seashells, starfish, and marine life to sand castles, sailing ships, and lighthouses. The only thing better than coloring these illustrations would be to slip this book into your pocket or beach bag and take it with you to the seashore! Now you can travel to your newly found retreat of peace and serenity whenever you'd like with this petite-sized collection of sophisticated artwork.

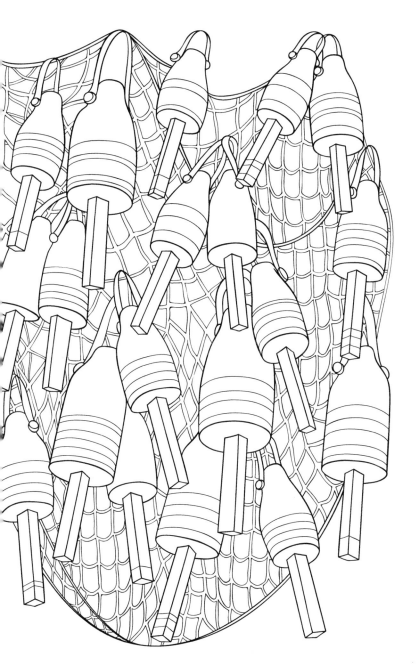

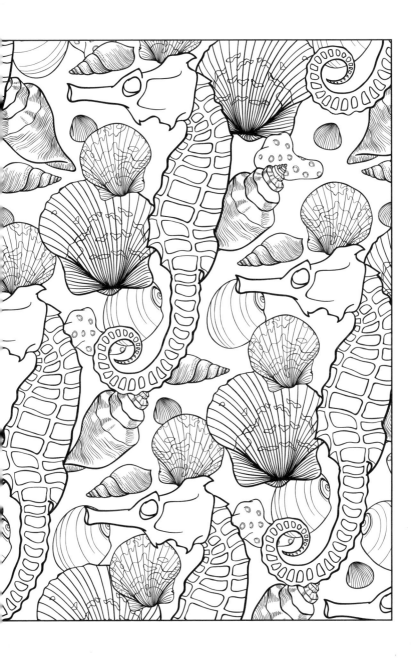